THE HEYDAY OF THE DMU

ALAN C. BUTCHER

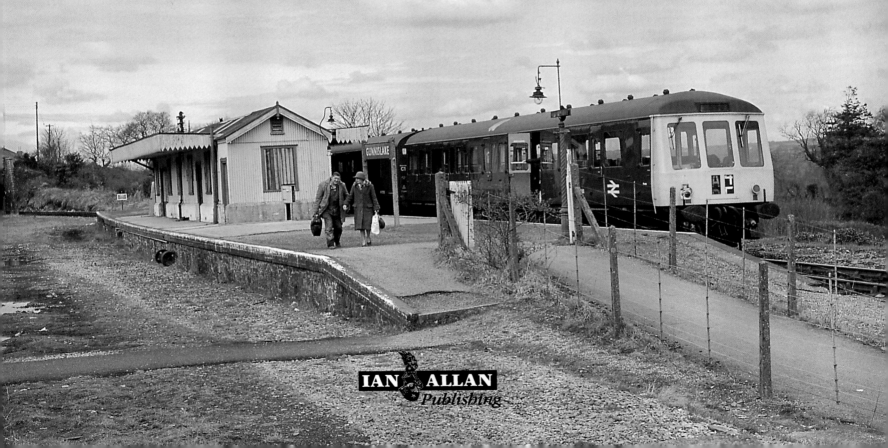

IAN ALLAN
Publishing

First published 1994

ISBN 0 7110 2319 0

Published by Ian Allan Publishing

an imprint of Ian Allan Ltd, Terminal House, Station Approach, Shepperton, Surrey TW17 8AS.
Printed by Ian Allan Printing Ltd Coombelands House, Coombelands Lane, Addlestone, Weybridge, Surrey KT15 1HY.

Alan C. Butcher has asserted his rights to be identified as Author and Designer of this work in accordance with the Copyright, Design & Patents Act 1988.

Dedication

For Charlotte who is far more interested in Mr Blobby than Diesel Multiple-Units

Front cover:
An unidentified Wickham two-car unit emerges from the deep Chappel cutting whilst working the 15.57 Sudbury-Colchester service. Regarded as oddities within the BR DMU fleet, the last Wickham units were withdrawn from traffic by 1972.
G. R. Mortimer

Previous page:
A scene which seems to sum up BR's attitude of the 1960s and 1970s. This Class 116 DMU has just arrived at Gunnislake, the present end of the truncated Callington branch, in 1971. Operated on a 'one engine in steam' basis, the long siding from Plymouth now sees more modern Sprinter units. *M. Pope*

Introduction

When asked to compile this colour album covering the heyday of the diesel multiple-unit (DMU) it posed a slight problem. Just when was the heyday? To many people this era probably did not exist.

In order to save arguments the author has set an arbitrary cut-off date of 1976. This year saw the first refurbished unit re-enter passenger service, and the start of development work on what was to become the second generation DMU; which, by early 1994, had reduced the 'traditional' unit almost to extinction on BR metals.

The introduction of the DMU in the mid to late-1950s heralded the demise of the steam-powered branch line train. To the travelling public this was probably no bad thing; as traffic levels tended to increase, resulting in some cases of overcrowding and reversion to the 'bad old days' of steam. Alas the 1960s saw Dr Beeching's report. This resulted in the death knell of the branch lines, but as Dr Beeching's axe swung, it cut not only the unremunerative branch but much of the trunk as well. Then with the excess of DMUs more of the steam-worked main line system saw the change to multiple-units; and in a few cases the demise of the units themselves. The overall result was that the DMUs were seen as the villains of the piece country wide, seeing off everybody's favourite steam classes.

The largest proponent of diesel units in the pre-Nationalisation days was the Great Western Railway with its fleet of railcars and the parcel-carrying variants. These plied the main lines out of Paddington, as well as lightly-used branch lines around the London suburbs and the West Midlands. Over the years they proved to be reliable forms of transport, and led the way for the introduction of their BR descendants in the 1950s.

Early BR ideas were in the form of four-wheel railbuses, with seven British United Traction Co vehicles entering service in 1952. No more-two axle railbuses entered traffic until 1958 when 22 examples were put into stock. These were built by several British manufacturers, and five were even imported from Germany in the shape of the Waggon & Mäschinenbau examples. It was claimed that these were for use on branch lines that could not be operated profitably using the 'new' types of DMUs then entering service. However, with the loss of the lines they worked on, these railbuses were withdrawn within 10 years, the last remaining in traffic only until early 1968.

What we have now come to regard as 'traditional', or 'heritage', units were introduced from the middle of the 1950s. The 'Modernisation Plan' era on BR provided a final boom period for British manufacturers of rail traction vehicles. This industry built some 2,000 vehicles over the next few years, which entered traffic alongside the BR-built examples. Private manufacturers included such well known names as Metropolitan-Cammell, Birmingham RC&W, Gloucester RC&W, along with the not quite so well known (at least as traction builders) Cravens and Pressed Steel.

Right:
Gloucester single car unit (later Class 122) at Penarth on 8 July 1967. Rationalisation is evidenced by the buffer stops behind the unit which was to form the 12.05 shuttle to Cadoxton. *Hugh Ballantyne*

The early BR DMUs were not always the most reliable form of traction. A number of types suffered, along with diesel locomotives, from having to be serviced alongside steam locomotives. British Railways possessed few qualified diesel or electric fitters when the modernisation programme was started. The result being that it was left to the likes of the Shed Masters and District Locomotive Inspectors to muddle through, overseeing not only the introduction of the vehicles, but encouraging the shed staff to develop new skills to maintain the units in traffic.

History has shown that the hard-pressed staff succeeded in maintaining the services, but at what cost is hard to quantify.

The illustrations within this album have been chosen in order to give what I hope to be a country-wide view of this period. In 80 pages it is difficult to show every branch or main line; or indeed, every class or type of vehicle. Although class numbers were not used until well after introduction of these units where-ever possible details are included in the captions for ease of reference.

Alan C. Butcher
Scarning
May 1994

Acknowledgements
I would like to thank the following photographic contributors for searching out suitable illustrations for use within this book; without their valued assistance the compilation of this title would have been more difficult: Ron White (Colour-Rail), Hugh Ballantyne, Michael Mensing and Chris Gammell.

Right:
A Metro-Cammell-built Class 101 forms the 17.40 Newcastle-Tynemouth via Benton Manors service on 16 July 1976. Nice roof and weathering detail for the modeller.
D. A. Robinson

A view that presents the end of the era to be covered in this volume. A refurbished Class 101 unit stands at Ayr in January 1975.

Several units were experimentally modernised to arrive at a cost effective result. *The late Derek Cross*

Pre-Nationalisation Pioneers

Left:
The original AEC/GWR design was for a streamlined single car unit as witnessed by No W14 at Birmingham Snow Hill in April 1958. The BR livery of carmine and cream gave these vehicles a 'lighter' look than the original GWR livery.
T. J. Edgington/Colour-Rail (DE483)

Right:
It emerged that the single cars did not have the capacity for some services so two-car sets were developed. A refinement was that a 'normal' coach could be added to strengthen the set further if required as can be seen here at Landor Street junction in 1955. The set with diesel vehicle Nos W33/38 was on a special working. *C. Banks collection/Colour-Rail (DE1565)*

Below right:
As well as the passenger-carrying examples the GWR also a parcels variant. No W34 is seen in action at Southall in April 1953. This vehicle remained in service until displaced by its BR equivalent. *T. B. Owen/Colour-Rail (DE651)*

Four-Wheel Railbuses

No 77661 was a member of the five Waggon & Maschinenbau-built railbuses. These vehicles represented the only real attempt by BR to draw on overseas multiple-unit experience during the Modernisation Plan era. They were also the only railbuses that could be worked in multiple having buffers and proper drawgear fitted, however, two drivers were required as no multiple-unit control gear was fitted (scarcely economical in view of the cost savings envisaged). The usual problem with a small fleet of non standard vehicles was encountered: the lack of spares back up. As a result three vehicles had their original Buessing engines replaced by AEC examples. Used in East Anglia, No 79961 is seen at Bartlow on the service from Audley End on 8 April 1961. *Chris Gammell*

The Park Royal-built four-wheel railbuses could be recognised by the two-figure train description panel, two marker lights and, a roof-mounted headlight. A notable feature of these vehicles was the long overhang of the body, unfortunately not visible in this view of an unidentified example leaving Knockando on the Aviemore-Craigellachie line, 14 July 1959. The five Park Royal vehicles were initially allocated to the LMR and ScR, all ending their days in Scotland. *Chris Gammell*

9

Right:
Nicknamed 'Flying Bricks', this is a rare colour view of the privately-sponsored four-wheeled three-car multiple-unit railbus train. Built in 1952 by ACV (Sales) Ltd three sets were tried out on BR metals, and were finished in two-tone grey with red band. This snatched shot shows an unidentified set beetling off to Amwylch in 1953. The three sets were sold to BR for service on the LMR, and BR green livery was applied. It was claimed they were rough riding and uncomfortable; this fact probably explains their withdrawal in February 1959, although scrapping did not take place for another three and a half years. *W. G. Rear/Colour-Rail (DE941)*

Below right:
Looking more like a bus of the late 1950s, as opposed to a railbus, this somewhat over-stylized vehicle was one of two built by Bristol Commercial Vehicles with Eastern Counties bodywork. Both these Gardner-engined vehicles went to the Scottish Region where this unidentified example is operating the Lugton-Beith service in September 1962. These two vehicles had probably the best power-unit available at the time and operated quite well until the mass withdrawal of the Scottish railbuses in 1966. A careful look will reveal passenger numbers at the time—zero! *B. Patton/Colour-Rail (DE653)*

The first of the five types of railbus to operate on BR metals, in February 1958, was the AC Cars example. Built by Associated Commercial Cars (hence AC Cars) of Thames Ditton, a firm normally specialising in road vehicles, many components were compatible with the rest of the BR fleet of DMUs and the bus industry of the period. When built the vehicles were delivered to AEC's works at Southall and trials were undertaken on the Brentford branch. No proper buffing or drawgear was fitted as the type was not expected to haul loads or work in multiple. No 79976 is seen at Tetbury of 7 March 1964 preparing to work the 2.15 to Kemble. This vehicle now survives at County School where a comprehensive rebuild to operating condition is to be undertaken following its withdrawal from traffic by BR more than 25 years ago. *Hugh Ballantyne*

Independent Builders

The Cravens Railway Carriage & Wagon Co of Sheffield was more used to supplying locomotive-hauled stock than self-propelled units. However an order for 405 vehicles was received in the mid-1950s. The Cravens units gained a bad reputation once in service for producing vibrations akin to 'rattling or shaking themselves to pieces'. Within the order there were a number of variations. Whilst most became Classes 105 or 106, 25 two-car sets were fitted with Rolls Royce engines and hydraulic torque converters, as illustrated here. This permutation caused nothing but trouble, indeed a number of vehicles suffered fire damage over the years. As a result all the Rolls Royce/torque converter vehicles had been withdrawn by 1970. This view illustrates the 12.23 Barrow-Preston service at Grange-over-Sands on 21 June 1968. *Michael Mensing*

The firm of D. Wickham & Co of Ware, Hertfordshire, had built a considerable number of small permanant way trolleys for Britain's railways over the years and contributed five two-car sets to BR for evaluation. Their integral construction, which would cause repair problems in the event of accident damage did not endear them to BR hearts. Introduced in 1957 and allocated to East Anglia, two sets were withdrawn in 1965 and sold to Trinidad, a third set was withdrawn in 1967 and, after a number of years in store, was converted to a saloon for the Eastern Region's General Manager. The two other sets survived until 1969/72. The ER saloon survived to be preserved. The set seen here at Fordham Junction is working the Mildenhall branch service in June 1962. Note the malachite green livery, complete with whiskers, and the deep vermilion-painted buffer beam. *Colour-Rail (DE1425)*

With No 79066 nearest the camera, this set was one of the first 36 two-car DMUs ordered from Metropolitan-Cammell. Similar in specification to the 'Derby Lightweights' these vehicles entered traffic in 1955, being allocated to East Anglia (29 sets) and the LMR for the Bury-Bacup route. The units set the style for all the Metropolitan-Cammell-built DMUs, which to a certain extent Derby Works followed for later steel-bodied builds. Whilst successful these vehicles were withdrawn from service as the lines they operated were deleted from the BR network. Being non-standard in terms of multiple-unit control equipment also limited their usefulness elsewhere. The two-car set is seen at Aldeburgh on 10 September 1966.
Chris Gammell

These Gloucester RC&W units were a variation on the original Derby two-car sets, and were of a 'semi-lightweight' nature. Events conspired to overtake these units in terms of body construction, although the mechanical layout was acceptable, and later Gloucester builds were based on BR's own specification (see Class 119). The 09.28 Seaton-Stamford service is shown here on 28 May 1966 approaching Marcott Tunnel. *Michael Mensing*

Left:
Todays Class 101 is an amalgam of several batches of basically similar Metropolitan-Cammell designs, ordered over a period of four years. Numerically the class totalled 637 vehicles, of which 364 were power cars. These vehicles consist of an integral body design similar to the original Met-Cam 'lightweights', but a lot stronger and heavier; for structural strength and collision resistance the body ends are steel. With through gangways within each two, three or four-car set and toilet facilities the units are suitable for long distance runs. The fuel capacity also allowed through weekend excursions. Vehicles Nos 51181 and 56337 are seen here working the 13.18 Gobowen-Oswestry shuttle service at Park Hall Halt on 30 August 1966. *Hugh Ballantyne*

Above:
An example of the use of Class 101s on excursions is illustrated with the RCTS 'Cotswold Edge' railtour on Saturday 21 November 1970. The three-car unit consisted of vehicles Nos 50304, 59115 and 50338, based at Tyseley. The itinerary started at Birmingham New Street and visited Gloucester, Worcester, Cheltenham and Stratford-upon-Avon, returning to Birmingham. The tour is seen here at High Orchard, Gloucester. *Hugh Ballantyne*

Above:
The Class 101 unit's bogie design was a single-bolster arrangement that did not give the best of rides but, overall, the units were one of the most successful designs. Here two units on Glasgow-Stirling services pass at Cadder Yard on 16 April 1971. *The late Derek Cross*

Right:
Another RCTS railtour to see the use of Class 101s was the 'Somerset Quarryman' on 28 September 1974, although in the event no quarry lines were traversed. The start was again Birmingham New Street, running to Bristol, Westbury, Frome, Hapsford (the connection for Whatley Quarry) and the East Somerset Railway at Cranmore where the photograph was taken. *Hugh Ballantyne*

Left:
It was a Met-Cam Class 101 that was chosen to demonstrate the refurbishment proposals which were announced in 1974. It was planned to refurbish units that were expected to be in service after 1980, and work included new seats and upholstery, floor and wall coverings, fluorescent lighting, modified heating system, engine mountings plus other alterations. As well as internal alterations a new livery went with it to differentiate between 'old' and 'new' units. Whoever chose a white livery for railway service? A refurbished Class 101 unit stands at Oban on 27 June 1975. The unit will form the 18.55 to Glasgow. *G. A. Watt*

Above:
The Class 101s were seen virtually all over the country: this is Whitley Bay on 4 September 1976 as a four-car unit departs with the 13.15 to Newcastle via Wallsend. *D. A. Robinson*

Left:
The firm of Park Royal is more associated with road vehicles but, as recounted earlier, was involved with the GWR railcars in association with AEC/Hardy Motors. In the early 1950s Park Royal was involved with the four-wheel railbuses and it was understandable that it would tender for some of the huge numbers of DMUs required by BR. The result, in 1957, was the Class 103s. In general appearance they followed the 'Derby Lightweights' but differed in details — the use of a two digit route number panel, two marker lights and a more sympathetic front end design. The bodywork of these units proved troublesome resulting in early withdrawal despite being compatible in terms of control equipment with the rest of the BR DMU fleet. Vehicles Nos 50413 and 56169 are seen here doing the 'honours' on the last day of services on the Belmont branch with the 11.20 to Harrow, 3 October 1964. *Hugh Ballantyne*

Below:
As the Class 103 units were concentrated on the London Midland and Western Regions it is somewhat apt that a unit should be illustrated on a former GWR line that came to be operated by the LMR. An unidentified unit is at Harlech in July 1967, with a nice Snowdonia backcloth. *C. L. Caddy/Colour-Rail (DE1184)*

Above:
The 17.15 Rugby (Midland)-Birmingham New Street service was operated by a Class 103 on 26 May 1966, which is seen here to the west of Berkswell & Balsall Common.
Michael Mensing

Built by the Birmingham Railway Carriage & Wagon Co the Class 104 units entered traffic in 1957. This was one of the more successful designs of the period. The front ends had the cab windows raised which resulted in the curved lining bands as seen here. Whilst distinctive in green livery, BR plain blue did nothing for the vehicles' looks. This three-car set was seen at Southminster on 6 September 1969, it is interesting to note that the centre vehicle has received BR plain blue whilst the driving vehicle retains its green paint scheme. *Chris Gammell*

25

Above:
We move into the all-blue era at Buxton on 23 March 1973. With vehicle No 50427 leading a three-car set prepares to leave with the 11.45 to Manchester Piccadilly. *Hugh Ballantyne*

Right:
An unidentified three-car Class 104 unit rolls into Blythe Bridge station on 15 May 1974 with a Crewe-Derby service. The distinctive North Staffordshire Railway signalbox was not to survive following the resignalling of the route. *Hugh Ballantyne*

Left:
Selby station on 25 May 1974. A four-car Class 104 unit loiters in platform 1, DMC No 50566, being nearest the camera. A Class 101 set bound for Hull occupies platform 2. *Chris Gammell*

Above:
As mentioned earlier Cravens received an order for 405 vehicles which went on to become Classes 105/106. Although more reliable in terms of mechanical features, body rattle did not endear them to the travelling public. The Cravens units were used on duties to which they were not really suited. With the closure of the rural branch lines the almost new units were sent to do battle with the heavy commuter traffic into King's Cross. The units were not suitable for dense-loading commuter traffic, with only two bodyside doors per carriage, bus-type seating and formed in multiples of six or eight (with all those empty driving cabs). Some units managed to escape and on 28 August 1973 we see the 15.39 service from Miln Row to Oldham at Miln Row. *Hugh Ballantyne*

Below:
Another 'country' set is seen here on 18 September 1975 with a two-car set leaving Great Yarmouth for Norwich. Following withdrawal by BR three Cravens units saw further service on the West Somerset Railway. *Hugh Ballantyne*

Right:
Just to confuse the unwary, not all destinations carried by the DMUs matched the service being operated. On 29 July 1970 this Class 105 set was operating the 07.52 Marks Tey-Sudbury working, despite bearing Colchester on the blind. The two-car set is seen crossing Chappel viaduct. *G. R. Mortimer*

Left:
The Class 110s were the last DMUs built by the Birmingham RC&W before its demise. Generally similar to the Class 104s, changes were made to the front ends to accommodate four-character route indicators and Rolls Royce engines were fitted. The latter was to give a few extra horse power for the difficult routes these units were to operate over. On 13 October 1961 the 9.50am Middlesbrough-Scarborough service was photographed nearing Sleights.
Hugh Ballantyne

Right:
The six-car Class 110 set seen here is the 16.33 Harrogate-Leeds-Manchester (Victoria)-Liverpool (Exchange) service on 17 July 1965. The location is the closed station at Arthington.
Michael Mensing

Above:
Similar to Met-Cam's Class 101 units, the Class 111s were fitted with Rolls-Royce engines giving more power than the BUT or Leyland ones fitted to the '101s'. The two classes were totally compatible and used indiscriminately, the only differences being in detail and difficult to tell apart except by the numbers and a slight cab window variation. The set seen here in June 1957, with No 59063 leading, is virtually brand new and is passing Longsight on its way to Manchester.
W. Oliver/Colour-Rail (DE938)

Right:
These Pressed Steel-built vehicles were for the WR's suburban service. Similar to the Derby high-density units the order was placed with Pressed Steel as a matter of expediency, the BR workshops having full order books at the time. Built as non-gangwayed vehicles passengers were in the driving coaches were isolated from the toilets in the centre trailer. The units were subsequently refurbished, complete with gangways, to increase their intended life-span into the late 1980s. This view was taken during the course of the RCTS 'Thames & Avon' railtour on 6 April 1968. The three-car Class 117 unit (Nos 51367/59513/51409) has been strengthened by the addition of a Class 101 vehicle (No 59543), thus illustrating the use of MU control system compatibility. The unit is seen leaving Radstock for the short run up to Writhlington Colliery, on the last surviving portion of the Somerset & Dorset Joint Railway at the time. *Hugh Ballantyne*

Below:
The Class 119 units were built by Gloucester RC&W in 1958 to Derby specifications which explains the BR family resemblance. When built the sets included buffet facilities but these were subsequently taken out of use and as with other types of unit they were moved around the Regions as traffic patterns changed and lines closed. The units proved successful and a small number are still in traffic. This view shows a set with the centre car removed leaving Yatton on the 17.46 service to Clevedon on 2 July 1966. *Michael Mensing*

Right:
This lovely scene was taken at Calstock station on the former Southern Region's 'Withered Arm' in June 1966, although by this date the service was operated by the Western Region. Of note is the casual dress of the signal woman who is receiving the single line token from the driver of the Class 119 unit. *Bill Chapman/Colour-Rail (DE1105)*

These Pressed Steel-built Class 121 vehicles were the BR equivalent of the original GWR/AEC single-car designs. With high density seating and no gangways, they were capable of hauling a tail load, or working in multiple with other units. With the 15 single-unit railcars Pressed Steel also delivered 10 non-powered driving trailers. No 55026 is leaving the single-coach length platform at Alberta Place on 6 May 1967, bound for Penarth. *Hugh Ballantyne*

A Class 121 single car is seen at Bourne End on the 11.24 High Wycombe-Maidenhead service in August 1966. With through services now but a memory Bourne End is still however the 'Junction for Marlow'.
Bill Chapman/Colour-Rail (DE1100)

Below:
The Gloucester RC&W Class 122 was the first type of single-car unit to enter traffic, built concurrently with the Class 119s they had the same power unit and other details but the passenger accommodation was to Derby high density standards, and there was a full-width driving cab at both ends. Initially allocated to the London Midland and Western Regions some later gravitated to Scotland. For use with these units Gloucester also built Driving Trailer Seconds (with cab at one end only) for use when passenger loads exceeded the capacity of a single unit, a practice of the former GWR. The first of the class, No 55000, is seen basking in the sun outside Swindon Works freshly delivered from the manufacturers in May 1958. As the following views will show, this is the neater end — no exhaust pipes!
RCTS/Colour-Rail (DE1333)

Right:
The Class 122s had a fair sized guard's compartment which is just as well seeing the amount of parcels on the trolley at Ironbridge & Broseley on 6 September 1963. The run down of the Bewdley-Shrewsbury route is evident from the state of the track and station nameboard, indeed the line closed three days later. Note that the exhaust pipes ruin the neat front end layout on No W55005.
Hugh Ballantyne

Above:
This view is of No W55019 at Lavernock on 8 July 1967. The line between Cadoxton and Penarth survived until May the following year. As can be seen the station was almost in the middle of nowhere, it is therefore surprising that it was not axed earlier. *Hugh Ballantyne*

Right:
The 16.47 Langley Green-Birmingham Snow Hill service was in the hands of a Class 122 on 5 August 1967 and was photographed as it left Smethwick and crossed the viaduct over both the canal and LNWR Stour Valley line. After electrification of the WCML and withdrawal of through services at Snow Hill, this service and an an hourly DMU via West Bromwich to Wolverhampton Low Level remained to serve Snow Hill. *Michael Mensing*

Left:
This was a purpose-built design of single-car parcels van by Gloucester RC&W, unlike the Cravens version (see opposite page) access was via three double doors each side. A trailing vacuum-braked load could be hauled and the class was compatible with the Blue Square system vehicles. Fitted with two 230hp engines when two cars were worked in multiple it gave one of the most powerful DMU formations possible. This unidentified vehicle is seen heading northbound at Spring Road, near Tyseley, on the north Warwickshire line on 26 June 1961.
Michael Mensing

Right:
Three of these Cravens single-car parcels vans were built, with driving cabs at each end and no gangway connections, they were capable of hauling a tailing load. Although similar in appearance to the Cravens-built two-car passenger sets, they could not work with them due to coupling code incompatibility, being Yellow Diamond. No 55999 is seen here passing Watery Lane box, Tipton, on the LNWR Stour Valley line on Sunday 30 July 1961. *Michael Mensing*

British Railways-Built

Below:

The Swindon-built Inter City units of 1956 were unique in a number of ways, for a start oil lamps had to be carried for tail end use! Destined for use on both Western and Scottish Regions, the undoing of these, the first express units, was the poor ride quality of the bogies compared to the locomotive-hauled coaches they replaced. When these units were termed 'Inter City' the brand named had yet to be adopted as a general marketing name for BR main line passenger services. This view shows a six-car unit at Birmingham Snow Hill — roof boarded throughout 'Birmingham, Gloucester, Newport, Cardiff' — in 1958. *T. J. Edgington/Colour-Rail (DE1422)*

Right:

Another unique feature on the first batch of Inter City units was the use of a gangwayed driving coach as illustrated. The working seen here is an example of these express units being put to good use. This is the 8.10am Birmingham (Snow Hill)-Carmarthen service passing through Widney Manor on its way to Stratford upon Avon via Lapworth on 6 July 1959. *Michael Mensing*

Left:
Even before the Modernisation Plan was announced in 1955, these Derby railcars had made their debut, as part of a policy devised by Chief Mechanical Engineer R. A. Riddles and his team. The British Transport Commission had opted for multiple-units in 1952, and Derby was given the job of design and construction at the Carriage & Wagon Works. Because of their aluminium bodies, short underframes and low weight these pioneer units soon became known as the 'Derby Lightweights'. Nos 77900/1 were single cars with driving cabs at both ends, the exhaust pipes can be seen carried up the front of the vehicle, which consisted of no less than six panes of glass. No 79901 is at Buckingham with the 1.30pm service to Banbury in August 1956; this line was one of the success stories of dieselisation — an increase of over 400% in passenger takings was recorded after the units were introduced. *T. J. Edgington/Colour-Rail (DE491)*

Below:
The 'Derby Lightweights' could be made up as either one, two or four-car sets, one of the advantages of fitting vehicles for multiple-unit working. One of the two-car sets built for service in Lincolnshire is seen here at Boston station in 1955 about to work the Grantham service. The total weight for a two-car set, one powered one trailing vehicle was 48 tons. Not bad for a passenger capacity of 123.
C. Banks Collection/Colour-Rail (DE940)

Below:
Below:
A two-car 'Derby Lightweight' unit trundles south from Carlisle on the LNWR main line bound for Keswick on 17 July 1965. The Yellow Diamond MU coupling code can be seen either side of the warning panel. *Michael Mensing*

Right:
A 'Derby Lightweight' unit patiently waits at Hayfield in October 1966 prior to working back to Manchester. The station sports a nice array of LMR maroon-coloured signs, This line survived the Beeching era only to close in January 1970. *Bill Chapman/Colour-Rail (DE1115)*

Above:
The 'Lightweights' suffered from bodywork problems and were non-MU compatible with later built units and as such withdrawal started in the mid-1960s as 'spare' stock from closures elsewhere were made available. Some vehicles survived long enough to be repainted into BR plain blue livery as seen here as a two-car set approaching Harrington forming the 13.45 Whitehaven-Carlisle service on 20 June 1968. *Michael Mensing*

Right:
This was the second batch of 'Derby Lightweight' design, they retained a short underframe but incorporated a later front end layout, looking more modern than the the initial batch. The Class 108s were included in the refurbishment programme and remained in traffic in the early 1990s. Here we see the 08.21 Llandudno Junction-Blaenau Festiniog service, just east of Blaenau Tunnel, running away from the camera on 30 May 1966. *Michael Mensing*

Left:
In September 1969 the photographer caught this Class 108 unit running in to Grantham station on its way to Skegness. A number of these units are now in the hands of preservationists.
D. R. Vickers

Right:
These Derby-built units come in the 'heavyweight' category and represent the first vehicles of the Modernisation Plan proper, with numbers in the series 50xxx (pre-Modernisation Plan vehicles were in the 79xxx series). The Class 114s represented a change to steel construction as the aluminium alloys previously employed proved troublesome. When introduced the class was destined for the Eastern Region's Lincoln area services.

This is Spalding Town station on 3 October 1970 with a Peterborough-Skegness train about to depart; withdrawal of the local services was about to take place.

In the author's opinion the plain blue livery did nothing to encourage passengers due to its drabness.
G. R. Mortimor

Left:
Chinley North Junction on 6 September 1976 sees a Class 114 operating the 16.15 New Mills-Sheffield service. The Class 114s were included in the refurbishment programme which was completed in the early 1980s. *D. A. Robinson*

Above:
For outer suburban services from Marylebone a fleet of high density four-car units was ordered. One of these sets, by now designated Class 115, is seen at Quainton Road on 26 May 1975. This was on a gala day at the adjacent steam centre and presented one of the few occasions that it was possible to travel between here and Aylesbury. Regular passenger trains had long disappeared from this stretch of line which remained open for freight traffic. *T. A. Bigley*

Left:
Mechanically the Class 116s reflected the then current attitude of Derby Works, with the standard bogies that gave a poor ride once wear set in. The use of numerous bodyside doors however was a new departure as these units were intended for surburban services. As it transpired there were numerous problems. No through gangway access to toilets (there weren't any!) also denied the guard or driver to help in an emergency, cramped seating, and the droplights in the doors created maximum draughts and minimum comfort. For short journeys the units were tolerable but, in usual BR fashion, the trips they were employed on were not short — is it any wonder customers preferred their own cars or other forms of public transport? It is also claimed that on occasions due to gross overloading that the body flexed under the weight and the doors could not be opened. On 29 April 1962 the last passenger trains from Blaenavon (Low Level) to Newport ran. The last train consisted of vehicles Nos 50842, 59328 and 50895 and is seen at Blaenavon.
Hugh Ballantyne

Right:
Ebbw Vale on 23 April 1962 and a Class 116 unit has arrived with the 1.05pm service from Aberbeeg. The class was included in the refurbishment programme, with some sets receiving gangway connections.
Michael Mensing

Left:
The driving coach leading this Class 116 formation, arriving at Whitlock's End Halt, is from an early batch as it does not possess the two figure headcode panel seen in the previous views. The six-coach set is operating the 10.35am Stratford upon Avon-Birmingham Snow Hill service on 8 July 1962.
Michael Mensing

Right:
When the Modernisation Plan was announced many cross country lines still figured in BR's network and it was decided that a special type of unit was required to serve this type of traffic. Swindon's thought returned to the early ideas of intermediate trailers incorporating buffet facilities, with within unit gangways. The design was similar to the earlier Inter City sets, although later-built driving coaches featured a four-figure headcode panel as illustrated in this view of a three-car set forming the 5.45pm Worcester (Shrub Hill)-Bromyard service near Suckley on 9 September 1961.
Michael Mensing

Right:
With Dr Beeching's economies taking hold the Class 120s were switched round resulting in them being used on the ER, WR and LMR, having originally been concentrated on the WR and ScR. Evesham on 14 April 1962 saw the 3.35pm Stratford-upon-Avon to Worcester/Ledbury service operated by a three-car set. *Michael Mensing*

Far right:
As mentioned before the early batch of the Class 120s were minus the four-digit headcode panel which gave a neater front end look, as can be seen in this view of the 5.55pm Bath (Green Park)-Mangotsfield-Bristol service leaving Oldland Common station on 13 May 1964. *Michael Mensing*

Left:
It took BR up until 1964 to come up with what was regarded as the best DMU design in terms of passenger comfort — the Swindon-built Inter City Class 123 — and, as is so often the case, they were the last new design to appear under the Modernisation Plan. The passenger accommodation was the equivalent of the best carriage design. The driving cabs were arranged with Pullman-type gangways to allow access through the entire train. As built a buffet car was included in the unit. Initially based on the Western Region, the units were later transferred to the Eastern to join the Trans-Pennine units. On 26 August 1964, about half a mile north of Barnt Green, the 17.20 Derby-Cardiff General was caught by the camera. When introduced the gangway connection cover was painted yellow.
Michael Mensing

Right:
Prior to the closure of the Taunton-Minehead branch there was a Saturdays Only through service from Paddington to Minehead. Having left the Capital at 08.50 the service was photographed as it rolled down the bank between Washford and Blue Anchor on 18 July 1970. The branch survives today as the West Somerset Railway, but no Class 123 vehicles escaped the scrapman.
Hugh Ballantyne

Living up to its tag of an Inter City unit, this impressive shot at Crewe was taken prior to the unit's departure as the 16.00 service for Cardiff on 26 May 1976. The Class 123 units survived in traffic until 1984. *T. A. Bigley*

Seventeen three-car Class 124 units were built for the fast Leeds-Liverpool service, entering traffic in 1960. The sets were intended to run as six-car units and as such each three-car unit possessed two power cars, one with a driving compartment, one without; this gave each six-car set a formidable 1,840bhp. The front end design was one of the most inspired, being in common with the same designer's Class 303/311 units. The units were not included in the refurbishment programme and are all now withdrawn. In happier times an unidentified unit is seen at Mirfield in September 1972. *J. Winkley*

The Class 126 consisted of the second batch of Inter City units, destined for the Scottish Region. As they had to be MU compatible with the first batch (see page 61) the White Circle coupling code had to be retained. The Edinburgh-Glasgow route on which they were initially used was to outgrow the unit's capacity and they were replaced by Mk 2 coaches and Class 27 locomotives. Latterly the units were concentrated upon the Ayrshire services, being based at Ayr itself. On 25 March 1970 a Glasgow-Girvan train is seen rolling into Ayr station. *The late Derek Cross*

Heading out of Glasgow Central, bound for Stranraer Harbour, this unidentified Class 126 unit is going about its daily duties. Being non-standard in terms of MU compatibility once the first batch was withdrawn in the early 1970s, it meant that the Class 126s were totally non-standard with the rest of the BR DMU fleet. The class however survived until the early 1980s with a three-car set surviving for preservation.
T. A. Bigley

Diesel-Electric Multiple-Units

Right:
The prestige trains of the Modernisation Plan
were the Metropolitan-Cammell-built 'Blue
Pullmans'. They set new standards of luxury
for British passengers with full air
conditioning, double glazing (with Venetian
blinds between the panes) and enclosed
gangway connections. The interior was the
result of a Design Panel study from mock-up
to finished train. A new livery of Nanking
Blue and white replaced the traditional
chocolate and cream of the locomotive-
hauled Pullman stock. One failing was the
unreliability of the North British/MAN
engines which resulted in the LMR and WR
each keeping one of their two units spare in
case of failure.

This view shows one of the WR's eight
car sets at Solihull in 1961, later the livery
was modified to include yellow ends prior to
repainting into the 'reversed' blue/grey Inter
City livery of later years. *Michael Mensing*

Right:
When BR adopted the blue/grey colour
scheme for its main line rolling stock it was
decided to re-livery the Pullman cars with a
'reversed' version which resulted in the
'Blue Pullmans' looking like this. As viewed
here the colour scheme did not maintain the
prestige image that the Pullman Co had built
up over the years; becoming very filthy very
quickly in day-to-day service. In 1969 the
LMR's sets were transferred to the Western
Region, lasting until the spring of 1973 when
all vehicles were withdrawn en-bloc. The end
was near when this eight-car set was
photographed at Bath whilst working a down
service from Paddington on 16 April 1973.
Hugh Ballantyne

In early 1955 new locomotive-hauled coaching stock was under construction for use on the Hastings line, designed specifically for the route, they were narrow-bodied and on 57ft underframes. A change of plan in April of that year saw authorisation for seven six-car diesel-electric multiple-units to enter service in 1957. The coaches under construction were incorporated into the order. An additional order for another 16 units were built on 63ft 6in underframes giving rise to two variations — long and short units!. The two power cars per unit incorporated English Electric 4SKRT engines, along with EE generator and motors. The Class 201 were built at Eastleigh Works where No 1005 is seen soon after completion. The 'slab' sides and short length of the vehicles can clearly be seen.
B. J. Swain/Colour-Rail (DE1525)

Some DEMUs were included in the modernisation plan for the Hampshire area of the Southern Region, the first batch of 18 two-car sets entering traffic in 1957. These were constructed to the normal BR loading gauge unlike the 'Hastings' units and the power equipment was the same as the 'Hastings' sets. This Class 205 two-car set, No 1122, was one of the second 'Hampshire' series and is seen leaving Itchen Abbas on 7 January 1968 with a morning Southampton-Alton service.
Michael Mensing

In 1962 a further batch of 26 three-car DEMUs were commissioned, seven for the Reading-Portsmouth service and 19 for the Oxted and East Sussex lines to work between Victoria and East Grinstead, Tunbridge Wells and Brighton via Uckfield. The Oxted units differed from the other batches by being built to 8ft 6in width instead of 9ft; this was due to restricted tunnel clearances at Tunbridge Wells. The centre vehicle contained a first class section and toilets which were located in the driving coaches of the earlier units. Class 207 unit No 1304 is seen at Honor Oak Park on 29 April 1968. *Chris Gammell*

Appendix

Multiple-unit number series as in use for 1968 which saw the greatest number of DMUs in service. Class numbers were not introduced until later but are included as additional information. Note that in all cases the Regional prefixes have not been included within the number series but shown under Regions allocated within the table.

Note: In 1983 units in the 50xxx and 56xxx series were renumbered into the 53xxx and 54xxx series respectively to avoid duplication of identities with locomotives under TOPS.

Diesel Multiple-Units

No series	Built	Type	Class	Regions Allocated	Notes
50000-049	Derby	MBS	114	E	2-car units
50050-091	Derby	MBS	116	M/W	Suburban 3-car
50092-133	Derby	MS	116	M/W	Suburban 3-car
50134-137	Met-Cam	MBS	111	E	2-car units
50138-151	Met-Cam	MC	101	E	4-car units
50152-157	Met-Cam	MBS	101	E	2-car units
50158-163	Met-Cam	MC(L)	101	E	2-car units
50164-167	Met-Cam	MBS	101	E	2-car units
50168-171	Met-Cam	MC(L)	101	E	2-car units
50172-197	Met-Cam	MC	101	E	4-car units
50198-233	Met-Cam	MBS	101	M	2-car units
50234-245	Met-Cam	MC(L)	101	E	4-car units
50246-248	Met-Cam	MBS	101	E	2-car units
50249	Cravens	MBS	105	E	4-car unit
50250-258	Met-Cam	MBS	101	E	2-car units
50260-269	Met-Cam	MC(L)	101	E	2-car units
50270-279	Met-Cam	MC(L)	111	E	3-car units
50280-292	Met-Cam	MBS	111	E	3-car units
50293-296	Met-Cam	MBS	101	E	2-car units
50297-320	Met-Cam	MBS	101	M	3-car units
50321-338	Met-Cam	MC(L)	101	M	3-car units
50339-358	Gloucester	MBS	100	Withdrawn	2-car units
50359-394	Cravens	MBS	105	E	2-car units
50395-414	Park Royal	MBS	103	M	2-car units
50415-419	Wickham	MBS	109	E	2-car units
50420-423	Birmingham	MBS	104	M	3-car units
50424-427	Birmingham	MC(L)	104	M	3-car units
50428-479	Birmingham	MBS	104	M	3-car units
50480-531	Birmingham	MC(L)	104	M	3-car units
50532-541	Birmingham	MBS	104	M	2-car units
50542-593	Birmingham	MC(L)	104	E	4-car units
50594-589	Birmingham	MBS	104	E	2-car units
50599-629	Derby	MBS	108	E	2 or 3-car units
50630-646	Derby	MC(L)	108	E	3 or 4-car units
50647-695	Swindon	MS(L)	120	W	Cross-Country 3-car units
50696-744	Swindon	MBC	120	W	Cross-Country 3-car units
50745-747	Met-Cam	MC(L)	101	E	3-car units
50748-751	Met-Cam	MC(L)	101	E	4-car units
50752-784	Cravens	MBS	105	M	2 or 3-car units
50785-817	Cravens	MC(L)	105	M	2 or 3-car units
50818-870	Derby	MBS	116	M/W	Suburban 3-car
50871-923	Derby	MS	116	M/W	Suburban 3-car
50924-935	Derby	MBS	108	M	2-car units
50936	Swindon	MS(L)	126	Sc	Inter City 6-car units
50938-987	Derby	MBS	108	M	2-car units
50988-1007	Derby	MS	125	E	Suburban 3-car
51008-029	Swindon	MS(L)	126	Sc	Inter City 6-car units
51030-051	Swindon	MBS	126	Sc	Inter City 3 or 6-car units
51052-079	Gloucester	MBC	119	M/W	Cross-Country 3-car units
51080-107	Gloucester	MS(L)	119	M/W	Cross-Country 3-car units
51108-127	Gloucester	MBS	100	Sc	2-car units
51128-140	Derby	MBS	116	M/W	Suburban 3-car
51141-153	Derby	MS	116	M/W	Suburban 3-car
51154-173	Derby	MBS	125	E	Suburban 3-car
51174-253	Met-Cam	MBS	101	M/E/Sc	2-car units
51254-301	Cravens	MBS	105	E	2-car units
51302-316	Birmingham	MBS	118	W	Suburban 3-car
51317-331	Birmingham	DMS	118	W	Suburban 3-car
51332-373	Pressed St	MBS	117	W	Suburban 3-car
51373-415	Pressed St	DMS	117	W	Suburban 3-car
51416-424	Derby	MBS	108	M	2-car units
51425-434	Met-Cam	MBS	101	E	2-car units
51435-470	Met-Cam	MBS	101	E/Sc	3 or 4 car units
51471-494	Cravens	MBS	105	E/Sc	2-car units
51495-504	Met-Cam	MC(L)	101	E	2-car units
51505-540	Met-Cam	MC(L)	101	E/Sc	3 or 4 car units
51541-550	Met-Cam	MBS	111	E	2 or 3-car units
51551-560	Met-Cam	MC(L)	111	E	2 or 3-car units
51561-572	Derby	MC(L)	108	M	4-car Suburban
51573-581	Swindon	MBC(L)	120	W	Cross-Country 3-car units
51582-590	Swindon	MS(L)	120	W	Suburban 4-car
51591-650	Derby	MBS	127	M	Suburban 4-car
51651-680	Derby	MBS	115	M	Suburban 4-car
51681-705	Cravens	MBS	—	M	2-car units
51706-730	Cravens	MC(L)	—	M	2-car units
51731-755	Cravens	MBS	—	M	2-car units
51756-779	Cravens	MC(L)	—	M	2-car units
51781-787	Swindon	MBC	120	Sc	Cross-Country 3-car
51788-794	Swindon	MS(L)	120	Sc	Cross-Country 3-car
51795-801	Met-Cam	MBS	111	Sc	3-car units
51802-808	Met-Cam	MC(L)	101	Sc	3-car units

No series	Built	Type	Class	Regions Allocated	Notes
51809-828	Birmingham	MBC	110	E	3-car units
51829-848	Birmingham	MC(L)	110	E	3-car units
51849-900	Derby	MBS	115	M	Suburban 4-car
51901-950	Derby	MBS	108	M	2-car units
51951-967	Swindon	MC	124	E	Trans Pennine 6-car units
51968-984	Swindon	MBS(K)	124	E	Trans Pennine 6-car units
51985-2010	Derby	MBS	107	Sc	3-car units
52011-036	Derby	MC(L)	107	Sc	3-car units
52037-065	Derby	MC(L)	108	M	2-car units
52066-075	Birmingham	MBC	110	M	3-car units
52076-085	Birmingham	MC(L)	110	M	3-car units
52086-095	Swindon	MBS(L)	123	W	Inter City 4-car
52096-105	Swindon	MS(K)	123	W	Inter City 4-car
55000-019	Gloucester	MBS	122	M/W	Single units
55020-035	Pressed St	MBS	121	W	Single units
55987-996	Gloucester	MPV	128	M	Parcels Van
55997-999	Cravens	MPV	129	M	Parcels vans
56000-049	Derby	DTC(L)	114	E	2-car units
56050-089	Met-Cam	DTC(L)	101	E/M	2-car units
56090-093	Met-Cam	DTC(L)	111	E/M	2-car units
56094-113	Gloucester	DTC(L)	100	M/Sc	2-car units
56114-149	Cravens	DTC(L)	105	E	2-car units
56150-169	Park Royal	DTC(L)	103	M	2-car units
56170-174	Wickham	DTC(L)	—	E	2-car units
56175-189	Birmingham	DTC(L)	104	M/E	2-car units
56190-215	Derby	DTC(L)	108	E/M/	2-car units
56218-220	Met-Cam	DTC(L)	101	NE	2-car units
56221-279	Derby	DTC(L)	108	M	2-car units
56280-289	Pressed St	DTS	121	W	2-car units
56291-299	Gloucester	DTS	122	M/W	Single unit trailers
56300-319	Gloucester	DTC(L)	100	Sc	2-car units
56332-411	Met-Cam	DTC(L)	101	M/E/Sc	2-car units
56412-483	Cravens	DTC(L)	105	E/Sc	2-car units
56484-504	Derby	DTC(L)	108	M	2-car units
59000-031	Derby	TC	116	M	Suburban 3-car
59032-041	Derby	TS	116	W	Suburban 3-car
59042-048	Met-Cam	TS	101	E	4-car units
59049-055	Met-Cam	TBS(L)	101	E	4-car units
59060-072	Met-Cam	TS(L)	101	E	4-car units
59073-085	Met-Cam	TBS	101	E	4-car units
59086-091	Met-Cam	TS(L)	101	E	4-car units
59092-097	Met-Cam	TBS(L)	101	E	4-car units
59098-099	Swindon	TBuF(L)	126	Sc	Inter City 3 or 6-car
59100-109	Met-Cam	TS(L)	101	E	3-car units
59112-113	Met-Cam	TBS(L)	101	E	4-car units
59114-131	Met-Cam	TC(L)	101	M	3-car units
59132-187	Birmingham	TC(L)	104	M	3-car units
59188-208	Birmingham	TS(L)	104	E	4-car units
59209-229	Birmingham	TBS(L)	104	E	4-car units
59230-234	Birmingham	TS(L)	104	E	4-car units
59235-239	Swindon	TS(L)	123	W	Inter City 4-car
59240-244	Birmingham	TBS(L)	104	E	4-car units
59245-250	Derby	TBS(L)	108	E	4-car units
59255-301	Swindon	TBuS(L)	120	W	Cross-Country 3-car
59302-306	Met-Cam	TS(L)	101	E	3 or 4-car units
59307-325	Cravens	TS(L)/TC(L)	—	M	3-car units
59326-376	Derby	TC	116	M/W	Suburban 3-car
59380-390	Derby	TS(L)	108	E	3 or 4-car units
59391-400	Swindon	TF(K)	126	Sc	Inter-City units
59402-412	Swindon	TC(L)	126	Sc	Inter-City units
59413-437	Gloucester	TBuS(L)	119	M/W	Cross-Country 3-car
59438-448	Derby	TC	116	M/W	Suburban 3-car
59449-468	Derby	TS	125	E	Suburban 3-car
59469-483	Birmingham	TC(L)	118	W	Suburban 3-car
59484-522	Pressed St	TC(L)	117	W	Suburban 3-car
59523-568	Met-Cam	TC(L)	101	E/Sc/W	3 or 4-car units
59569-572	Met-Cam	TS(L)	101	E	3-car units
59573-578	Met-Cam	TBuS(L)	111	E	4-car units
59579-588	Swindon	TBuS(L)	120	W	Cross-Country 3-car
59589-618	Derby	TS(L)	127	M	Suburban 4-car
59619-663	Derby	TS	115	M	Suburban 4-car
59664-678	Derby	TC(L)	115	M	Suburban 4-car
59679-685	Swindon	TBuS(L)	120	Sc	Cross-Country 3-car
59686-692	Met-Cam	TC(L)	101	Sc	3-car units
59693-712	Birmingham	TS(L)	110	E	3-car units
59713-718	Derby	TS	115	M	Suburban 4-car
59719-724	Derby	TC(L)	115	M	Suburban 4-car
59725-744	Derby	TS	115	M	Suburban 4-car
59745-764	Derby	TC(L)	115	M	Suburban 4-car
59765-773	Swindon	TS(L)	124	E	Trans-Pennine 6-car units
59774-781	Swindon	TBuF(L)	124	E	Trans-Pennine 6-car units
59782-807	Derby	TS(L)	108	Sc	3-car units
59808-817	Birmingham	TS(L)	110	M	3-car units
59818-827	Swindon	TC(K)	123	W	Inter City 4-car units
59828-832	Swindon	TBuF	123	W	Inter City 4-car units
79000-007*	Derby	MBS	—	Withdrawn	2-car units
79008-046	Derby	MBS	—	E/M	2-car units
79047-082	Met-Cam	MBS	—	E	2-car units
79083-111	Swindon	MBS(L)	—	Sc	Inter City 3 or 6-car units
79118-149	Derby	MBS	—	E/M	2-car units
79150-154	Derby	MS	—	Withdrawn	4-car units
79155-168	Swindon	MS(L)	—	Sc	Inter City 6-car units
79169-181	Derby	MBS	—	M	2-car units
79184-193	Derby	MC(L)	—	M	2-car units
79250-262	Derby	DTC(L)	—	Withdrawn	2-car units
79263-291	Met-Cam	DTS(L)	—	E	2-car units
79325-329	Derby	TBS(L)	—	Withdrawn	4-car units

Continued on page 77

Although carrying the comparatively modern BR all-over blue livery this Derby lightweight stands condemned at Carlisle Upperby in the summer of 1968. Scrapping followed the following year, probably on site together with the other units in this view.
Michael Mensing

Vehicle No 50476 leads this Class 104 set as it forms the 17.25 Derby (Midland)-Birmingham New Street service passing Wilmecote station on Sunday 22 April 1962.

Whilst the driver concentrates on the route ahead, the passenger in the seat behind seems to prefer a newspaper rather than enjoying the view. *Michael Mensing*

No series	Built	Type	Class	Regions Allocated	Notes
79400-404	Derby	TS(L)	—	Withdrawn	4-car units
79440-447	Swindon	TBuF(K)	—	Sc	Inter-City 3 or 6-car units
79470-482	Swindon	TF(K)	—	Sc	Inter-City 3 or 6-car units
79500-507	Derby	MC(L)	—	Withdrawn	2-car units
79508-512	Derby	MC	—	Withdrawn	4-car units
79600-632	Met-Cam	DTC(L)	—	E/M	2-car units
79633-684	Derby	DTC(L)	—	M	2-car units
79740	ACV (BUT)	MS	—	Withdrawn	3-car/4-wheel unit
79741	ACV (BUT)	TS	—	Withdrawn	3-car/4-wheel unit
79742-744	ACV (BUT)	MBS	—	Withdrawn	3-car/4-wheel unit
79745	ACV (BUT)	MS	—	Withdrawn	3-car/4-wheel unit
79746-747	ACV (BUT)	TS	—	Withdrawn	3-car/4-wheel unit
79748	ACV (BUT)	MS	—	Withdrawn	3-car/4-wheel unit
79749	ACV (BUT)	TS	—	Withdrawn	3-car/4-wheel unit
79750	ACV (BUT)	MBS	—	Withdrawn	3-car/4-wheel unit
79900-901	Derby	MBS	—	Withdrawn	Single units
79958-959	Bristol	Railbus	—	Withdrawn	4-wheel Railbus
79960-964	W&M	Railbus	—	Withdrawn	4-wheel Railbus
79965-969	Wickham	Railbus	—	Withdrawn	4-wheel Railbus
79970-974	Park Royal	Railbus	—	Withdrawn	4-wheel Railbus
79975-979	AC Cars	Railbus	—	Withdrawn	4-wheel Railbus

Battery-Electric Railcars (included as based on DMU bodywork)

No series	Built	Type	Class	Regions Allocated	Notes
79998	Derby/Cowlairs	MBS	—	Withdrawn	2-car units
79999	Derby/Cowlairs	DTC	—	Withdrawn	2-car units

Diesel-Electric Multiple-Units

No series	Built	Type	Class	Region Allocated	Notes
60000-045	Eastleigh	MBS	201/2/3	S	Hastings units
60100-121	Eastleigh	MBS	205	S	Hampshire 2 or 3-car units
60126-144	Eastleigh	MBS	207	S	East Sussex 3-car units
60500-561	Eastleigh	TS(L)	201/2/3	S	Hastings units
60600-618	Eastleigh	TC(L)	207	S	East Sussex 3-car units
60650-667	Eastleigh	TS	205	S	Hampshire 3-car units
60700-722	Eastleigh	TF(K)	201/2/3	S	Hastings units
60750-756	Eastleigh	TBu	201/2/3	S	Hastings units
60800-821	Eastleigh	DTC(L)	205	S	Hampshire 2 or 3-car units
60900-918	Eastleigh	DTS	207	S	East Sussex 3-car units

No series	Built	Type	Class	Regions Allocated	Notes
60090-093	Met-Cam	MBF(L)	—	W	Pullman 6-car units
60094-099	Met-Cam	MBF(L)	—	W	Pullman 8-car units
60644-649	Met-Cam	MBS(L)	—	W	Pullman 8-car units
60730-733	Met-Cam	MKF(L)	—	W	Pullman 6-car units
60734-739	Met-Cam	TKF(L)	—	W	Pullman 8-car units
60740-749	Met-Cam	TPF(L)	—	W	Pullman 6 or 8-car units

Key to Type

TBu	Trailer Buffet
TF(K)	Trailer First (Side Corridor)
TBuS	Trailer Buffet Second
TBS	Trailer Brake Second
TS	Trailer Second
DTC	Driving Trailer Composite
DTS	Driving Trailer Second
TC	Trailer Composite
MPV	Motor Parcels Van
MBS	Motor Brake Second
MS	Motor Second
MC	Motor Composite
(L)	Lavatory compartment within vehicle
TPF	Trailer Parlour First (Pullman)
TKF	Trailer Kitchen First (Pullman)
MKF	Motor Kitchen First (Pullman)
MBS	Motor Brake First (Pullman)
MBF	Motor Brake First (Pullman)

Back cover:
As well as diesel-mechanical multiple-units BR also possessed a number of diesel-electric examples. Mainly used on the Southern Region's unelectrified lines, they were based on EMU designs of the period. Class 205 'Hampshire' unit, No 1131, is seen here at Alresford on 4 February 1973; the last day of service 'over the Alps'. The Alresford-Alton section of the route now sees steam traction as the Mid-Hants Railway. *M. Pope*

Chinley North Junction sees a refurbished
Metropolitan-Cammell Class 101 unit
working the 18.07 New Mills-Sheffield
service on 6 September 1976. *D. A. Robinson*

The reader may well ask what a battery-electric multiple-unit view is doing in a book on DMUs, but a glance at this picture will reveal that whilst the traction power is different the styling is of a classic two-car

DMU. Built in 1958 and based on Derby-built bodyshells, the 'electrics' were the responsibility of Cowlairs. Nos 79998/9 remained in service until 1966, then entered Departmental Service prior to preservation.

The unit is seen at Aberdeen station whilst waiting to work to Ballater in May 1964.
R. Hill/Colour-Rail(DE332)

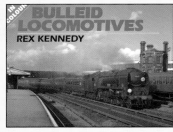